Honeycomb & Diamonds

J. Richard Wrigley

Honeycomb & Diamonds

Acknowledgements and Thanks

Some of the poems in this volume were first published, occasionally in earlier versions, in *The Weekend Australian*, *The Australian Poetry Journal*, *Penguin Days* (New Zealand Poetry Society anthology), *Valley Micropress* (NZ) and *Petrichor-Visible Ink 27* (RMIT anthology).

Sincere thanks to Judith Rodriguez for her generosity and guidance and to my wife Fiona, without whose loving encouragement and material support this work could not have come into being.

Honeycomb & Diamonds
ISBN 978 1 76041 333 0
Copyright © text J. Richard Wrigley 2017
Cover image: © vladi_mir - Fotolia.com

First published 2017 by
GINNINDERRA PRESS
PO Box 3461 Port Adelaide 5015 Australia
www.ginninderrapress.com.au

Contents

Honeycomb and Diamonds	9
Aran Isle Pullover	11
Innocent	13
Kirk Deighton	14
Free-thinker	15
Sunchair	16
That Mystic Eastern Stuff	19
Mites	21
Incense	22
Philokalia	25
Bhakti	26
Skill-in-means	27
The Blessings of TV	28
A Better Mousetrap	29
Bearer of Vessels	31
Ward Orderly	33
Leaving My Mark	35
Diaphanisation	36
Otuihau	37
Ways to Go	38
As from Trees in Autumn	41
Consanguinity	43
House of Confinement	44
Unique Voice	46
A Visit with My Father	48
Impermanence	50

One Grain of Sunblood — 51

- Prospecting — 53
- Blackbird, Stunned — 54
- Grand Final — 56
- Seven Balloons — 57
- Shade Tree — 58
- Smith Street — 59
- Sounds of Silence — 60
- Text Message — 61
- The Castle on the Hill — 62
- The Order of Birds — 63
- Title — 64
- Two Balloons — 66

A Bowl of Betrayal — 67

- Vineyard War Graves — 69
- In the Belly of a Giant Whale — 70
- By the Numbers — 71
- Prothesis in the Park — 73
- Renegade — 74
- Valorous — 75

Lunar Sea of Rhyme — 77

- Water of Life — 79
- On the Beach — 80
- Chrome-plating the Tail Fins — 81
- Semi-retired — 82
- Sacred Text — 84

Englamoured — 85

- Parent Birds — 87
- Sylvan Vision — 89
- Vajrayogini — 90

Four Balloons	91
Banshee	92

The Consequence of Line — 93

Chops	95
Fondue	98
Show Business	99
Green Grocer	101
Avant-garde Performance	102
Elation Muted	103
Sinophile	104

Schools of Style — 107

Stratigraphy	109
Delivery	110
Pursuit	112
At the Movies	113
River Red Gums	115

Honeycomb and Diamonds

Aran Isle Pullover

My grandmother knit me an Aran Isle
jumper, thick as two blankets, as warming
and tawny as a tumblerful of Scotch.
I had one already, worn layered during

Scots winters. Grandma's was larger by far,
a king's hefty ransom in golden wool.
She had taken months of time, skill and thought
for her opus and gave them all to me.

The sleeves, though, hung well beyond my fingers
and three or more as bulky could have fit inside.
Like Mummy's ball gown on a five-year-old,
good for dress-up, but of no earthly use.

I, her eldest and most distant grandchild,
never talked with her at length or in depth.
Dad told me, years later, when I first turned
East he had asked her what to do. Gazing

heavenward, she had said, 'Oh, as a girl
I had a spell of religious mania.
It was wonderful!'   I never knew.
Were her honeycombs and diamonds,

baskets and cables an Aran wife's wish
for safe harbour, fruitful labour and wealth?
Her maiden name Riley, was the jumper,
on the disputed border of orange,

tacit acknowledgement of the Irish descent
I wondered about but didn't once ask?
Had I thought my future children giants
the great woolly might have made an heirloom,

even so, headed for Tai Tokerau,
New Zealand, I had no need of it. There
was a man, tutor at the college, it
might fit. I found him pressed against a wall,

head on one side, as if the corridor
had shrunk. Offered gift and explanations
of misguessed size and emigration,
he accepted with a shrinking 'Thank you.'

More than I remember offering her.
Was it distance caused Grandma to see me
seven feet tall? How much less lofty that
than the mystery she presents me now: this

thoroughly English, putative daughter
of Erin; teetotal Methodist; elder
of five surviving Tommies, whose bawdry
always drew laughter from their strait-laced sis.

Innocent

My mother, seated in class
on time and clean, sees
another girl trudge in
in grass-seeded socks
and pullover stuck
with straw.
    Mum frowns judgement: Dirty.
Herself shamed by patches,
hand-me-downs, a room
shared with four brothers,
two sisters, and a flush
of relief, even pleasure,
    at one worse-off.
Blind to what the unflannelled
face and unbrushed hair might
mean, the lass's troubles:
whose attentions she struggles
to fend off; the kind of fate
she fights against, obligating
nights spent in a shed
amongst bales and cows.
Shocked to find herself arriving now
at a kinder, more mature
understanding, grateful for her own
trust inviolate, sad for condemning
a state of raw need,
understanding
arriving
decades late.

Kirk Deighton

I dream a beginning, a small boy scaling
    Ladder-like steps, his chin coming
        Level with my floor.

His hand so new, never before put
    To such a switch: a cord pulled, like the wave
        Of a wand, to light his eyes

And this, my attic space, now his for play.
    Walls and floor ascetic, bare. Shellacked,
        Tongue and groove breath, mingled

With 3-In-One oiled Hornby clockwork,
    Become the first scent inciting his delight
        In hours spent hermit-shelled in solitude.

Seized by dancing need left too late, he finds relief
    Kneeling at an O-scale railway water tank.
        Called to eat, he leaves the tin cup filled.

Days later his mother sniffs and frowns
    At what is stewing. Picks it up,
        Takes it out. He is shamed by her recital,

Slugs and snails and puppy dogs' tails.
    Only after years have passed and I long left
        To dust and drowse, will he learn

Of other failings wetly brewing, vital
    Pressures building and becoming
        More humiliating yet.

Free-thinker

My dad, ever the pragmatist, kept two
right-angled, galvanised rods in the boot
of his blue thirteen hundred.

Uniformed in monogrammed, one-piece overalls
and green rubber Wellington boots, he'd stalk
and routinely find lost polyethylene
plumbing; pipe laid buried under numbing
winter mud.

Unhurried, boots squelching,
he walked. I watched. The rods crossed
in his hands. He was good. Impressed, I asked how
he did it, why they turned. He scoffed
at my question, said, 'Anyone can dowse.'

One hot day the godawful stink of rot
coming from a humming hen Gehenna
prompted the speech: 'When you're dead you're dead.'
Not for him blind belief in the hereafter
or a tax exile, factory farmer's right
to ownership of mole grips and chrome
spanners.

Dafter not to bring good tools home
each night 'to stop them (wink) being stolen'.

Sunchair

The only time Mum had a black eye
it went through the usual changes: blue
through brown to yellow, gone in days. Try
as she might to explain, even I could see

people think, Only peasants, scum and drunks
beat their wives. Right enough, Dad had fallen
off the wagon, the one on which his mother
placed him as a babe in arms. Now

past forty, his Chapel-going days well
behind him, succumbing to the demon
drink: a glass of Harvey's Bristol Cream on
Christmas Eve and a Newcastle Brown

on Fridays, the bottle rinsed so Grandma, ninety
miles away, wouldn't know her baby
was halfway to Hell. The bruising however
caused by aluminium tubing,

clever hinges and plastic straps, yellow
and white, sunny sixties colours
like the formica in the kitchen. My parents'
sunchairs, back before the hole in the ozone,

when sunblock was tanning lotion and I,
at thirteen, was impressed by Ambre Solaire's
French sophistication. One rare day
Mum was setting up to bask in the garden,

kneeling on the bed, adjusting the back.
Her weight loading the ballista, the recliner
slipped her grip, snapped up and smacked
her, fist to head. The only time she wore a shiner.

That Mystic Eastern Stuff

Mites

Outside my room, the window frame and sill
a light blue paint that years of sun have bleached
chalk white. On that powdery pasture range
red mites, not quite minute enough to hide

from eyes, their carmine dye expressed by idle
thumbs, their minor murders carried out
in wonder, lacking thought for tiny lives.
Childish fun to find so much pigment pent

in specks so small. The milky surface spread
carelessly with crimson, a red too bright
for blood. The observation 'That looks like
cochineal' took time to penetrate. Slow

dawn of what the word connotes, moral sense
and comprehension of upon what hard
truth the little bottle in the larder
might depend. The Loon Fung's one-litre pack

of own-brand sweet and sour sauce displays,
not as it might, 'Ingredient: essence of arthropod'
or 'Mites: one gross per gram', but
'E120'. Infinitesimal creatures

engaged in seeking fulfilment of wishes,
food and mate, only to meet
a rude end colouring meatless dishes.
Vegetarian virtue rendered vicious.

Incense

Good Friday host, hallowed smoke
    loosed to swell into vaulted air.
Aroma, folded in
    mouldering hymnals
And beeswax, evoking
    an hallucinatory son et lumière
Of Sunday school,
    kneeling at prayer
In Anglican pews
    and Gothic ghost tales,
Waking, soaked and inconsolable,
    under His Holy, inescapable glare,
And bells:
    the village pealed afloat
A billowing tide of bellowing,
    change-ringing bells.

That thrilling swell aside,
    the feeling
Upwelling from a pall
    of parched resin,
Unappealing;
    foreign as a muezzin call.

Already hooked at first breath,
    teen in an English town,
On a line of scent, more sweet,
    spooled out from a
        source unguessed,
The lure of the Mystic East
    sent pouring, floral, down
        a northern shopping street.

Reeled in on a thread
    more fine than thought,
Blessed and empowered
    to escalating hours spent
Statuesque before
    an all-absorbing altar.

Clouds of juniper, sandal-
    and cedarwood,
Sufficient to shroud
    the Himalayas,
        sent ceilingward
Till walls kippered
    and gold glowered.

*

Sandalwood still sways each day
    in scented votive dance
Before a shrine, grown lama dancer high,
    longtime cell companion
In brocade and burgundy,
    freighted down the mountain,
Domesticated. Devotions made,
    in sight of kind,
Enshrined, unageing,
    gilt-framed faces.
Fragrance scant and fleeting.
    Pilot light ascesis.

Philokalia

Andrew enthused about a man he'd met
who had just come back from the Greek islands.
'He's into Gnosticism,' my friend said.

I was curious. We went to his place.
On the floor of an empty room his bed
lay folded round a mattress, neat as a

Japanese gift. On a table one book
lay closed. Freed of mundane concerns, the need
to speak or smile, I felt he nonetheless

bore the burden of his existential
quest. The impression remains, though I saw
him only once, of self-taught ascesis

kept pure in pursuit of the good and true.
His single bed, the simple clothes he wore,
white, as were the walls of his fourth floor cell.

In his eyes the same craving, diamond-bright,
the same scorched and sightless stare as one lured
too close and consumed, moth-like, by the light.

I too have glimpsed the real, but shied away,
instantly convinced the adamantine
shards of light too bright to bear would shred this

'I', the ordinary me. Did his zeal
for shedding self-deception endure or,
daring, like mine, too much, decline and die?

Bhakti

Pulling into a Coromandel street
in our HG Holden, I park the car
stop the motor and step out to Sanskrit.
The rhythmic chant Om Namah Śivāya

and a crusty bakehouse aroma share
the air, white-dusted louvres wide open.
Inside the baker – his labour a prayer –
leavens aloud his dough with devotion.

Skill-in-means

Chinese Doctor Bob and I escort our
guest to the car, parked outside the small town
polytech campus. On the way we pass
one who, caught by some drama in his head,

staggers blindly in the dark. He lunges
at the Lama. I see red, move to fend
him off and might yet descend to worse, but
for Bobby who, invoking the sacred

Himalayas, diverts his energy
saying gently, 'Our friend is from Tibet.'
Magic syllables to quell the stranger's
miasmatic wildness. His disturbance

subdued, no longer a danger, he slurs,
'Mount Ararat!' then stumbles on to seize
the robed one by the hands. Bob's mastery
patently in keeping with the evening's

teachings, I can only stand and watch
humbled and impressed by an expert
acupuncturist's kindness, his command of when,
where and which gold-plated word to insert.

The Blessings of TV

No predicting what pages, picture or
perfume might smuggle the message through,
what means the still small voice might use for
communication.   Garrie had Doctor Who,

actors in pratimoksha drag, chanting
basso profondo. Squatting on the floor
of a BBC studio Buddhist
temple, urging a mandala to morph,

bidding arachnoid aliens, big as
eight-legged borzois, swarm through a portal
to storm Swinging London.   Now he wears
burgundy robes himself.   For me the form

of a safari-suited, trouble-shooting
Jesuit did the trick. A sixties drama
of a monastic community in
the midst of conflict.   He sits like a lama

for one brief scene.   The priest in sukhāsana
more subversive than what he's come to snuff.
    Nag champa agarbathi, Ram Dass and…ah,
    but I love that mystic Eastern stuff.

A Better Mousetrap

As solution for mouse turds in the kitchen
I take a sturdy wooden box, cut an opening,
fix a mousetrap inside, not to kill but,
with a stiff length of wire from the spring-
loaded bar, pull a trick door shut.

The plastic lid of a broken record player
by chance a perfect fit as ceiling for the cell.
Pleased with my work I prime the trap,
put it under the hot water cylinder
and wait. Not much later, 'clack.'

Proud, I carry the device to my Holden
and drive, the offender on the red
vinyl bench seat boxed beside me,
persistently launching itself head
first against see-through polystyrene.

I stop the car in a playing field
a kilometre away and look. No let up.
The muzzle of my prisoner bleeding
more severely with each impact.
Cringing, I wish for an end to this thing.

Rap after bloody rap as I carry the box
to place it on the ground. I lift the lid,
step back and let the creature run, quick
to lose itself in grass. The mouse's spirited
response leaves me shocked. Feeling sick,

I stand over the contraption considering
my culpability for the forcible
removal of a parent, how its brood are soon
to be in acute need of food, how its wounds
would, if human, warrant an emergency room.

I take home my mousetrap whose exquisite
non-violence I vow not to revisit.

Bearer of Vessels

Ward Orderly

'The old man has passed away,' she says;
Sister, in her silver-buckled belt,
frilled cap and starched white linen apron,
inquiring, would I like to help.

Keen-eyed, though kindly,
she registers my dread,
offered this work, this role.
These offices of laying out the dead

to be undergone, the solemn rite
an initiation I, bearer
of vomitous vessels, must endure
in order to profess myself carer

for the sick. What lies tabernacled
in the corner bed, beyond the screen
behind the nurses' desk? Leading
through curtains she asks if I've seen

a corpse before. 'My grandfather,'
I say, feeling again my distaste
for his hands' waxen arrangement,
recalling his mask-like face,

unnaturally still, like the tenant
of this tented sheet. She draws the veil
away from the deceased to reveal
the vacancy, the livid grey

cadaver, too vivid, too real.
Chilled, my hands shake.
Sister gentles me through
the task we together undertake.

'Rolled to be washed, he may gasp,'
she warns. The limb I have to lift –
must force myself to grasp –
is stiff and cold. I cannot shift

the notion he may lunge, till,
witnessing the impotence of empty
eyes to smart, of soap to sting, I start
to value the lesson the departed

has gifted me with, that he, unlike
the late-night movie ghouls filling my head
as a youth, is as likely as a tree
once felled is to move. The old man is dead.

Leaving My Mark

A man came early one Sunday
To my Emergency Room, his injury
A gash to the head from the night before.
I assumed he, ashamed, had delayed
Presenting until sober.
Showered, but betraying
The state in which he fell,
He had, I felt,
A shamefaced look, regret
He'd lost control again, a ketone smell
And the aura of one reformed,
If only for the week.
Odd to learn later that, in the time I had
Spent speculating, he had held one thing
I did not know unsaid. He, whose
Details I had written down, and into
And onto whose skin, no doubt,
Thirty years on, still scarred,
I had sutured and knotted 5-O nylon thread,
Was the brother of my father's then lover.
How rich is the web, him almost kin,
Our meeting. And all I dare claim to recall
As hard fact, his hair, still wet, and him
Silently in stitches.

Diaphanisation

Asked urgently to donate, he rushes in,
willing, heroic. Lab technicians place him
on a creaking, base hospital table,
needle and relieve him of blood

for a neonate's refilling.
After giving, about to leave, he sees,
on the window ledge, someone's kin
suspended, a tiny, alizarin

death's head and hyphenated frame,
revulsion upwelling at flesh transgressed.
He has seen Surgeons' Hall Museum,
the work of Scots dissectionists

preserved, legions displayed in tanks
of formalin. Safe at a sepia distance
the yellowing ranks left him less disturbed
than sight of this one vivid foetus,

soft tissues pellucid as polar air.
Drawn closer to its station on the sill,
he, as jarred as it, can only stare.
Transparency, refracting like glass, clothing

crimson bone. Every downy swirl and pore,
perfect. Innocence caught gazing,
breathless, on the moment
of its own annihilation.

Otuihau

Drive out of town to where cow paddocks start.
Park on the car park's gravel. Heed the signs
that say leave nothing of value. Walk down
and step out on water-smoothed rock among

local kids neck-deep in dairy run-off.
Approach the edge with caution, lean over
and feel your stomach flip as the river
drops away. Take care on the path downward,

slick amidst thick, damp bush. Breathe the loamy
aroma. Once there look up at the wall
of hexagonal basalt curtained with
creepers. Feel the cold mist blown in your face,

hear the cataract thunder. Squint up at
the daredevil, silhouetted against
the sky as he havers, summoning the
courage to leap. Follow his flailing fall,

cringe at the skin-stinging smack. Hear his mates'
Tarzan call hailing his prowess. When his
head comes up remember to breathe. Recall
also the German who, swimming here, had

six rough feet of lumber plunge through his leg.
Ask if he who threw it, like the tourist,
came good, or if the boy who risked killing
stands still in thrall to a bourne of spilled blood.

Ways to Go

I remember a man slumped in a wheelchair
on the orthopaedic ward, that clinical space
of necessity his long term home.
He had no legs, no interest in prostheses

and a terrible cough. Years earlier
he had lain on the town's one railway track
intending himself dead. Hospitalised in a funk
ever since, he dwelt in a four-bedded room

at the lean end of the ward, opposite
a windowless boneyard of stored traction splints, rails
and frames, baskets of pulleys, ropes and weights.
A horde of youthful, motorcycling males

came and went, he sat and smoked. For the years
I nursed there, another man, old and frail,
shared the room. Neither spoke. More than once
I pushed Mr Edwards on a commode chair down

the vinyl in an open backed gown, sidestepping
his soft leavings. On the same busy corridor
an accountant, paralysed but still working full time,
had a single room with a good store of grog.

His custom furniture and big TV paid for
by compo when a rugby tackle left him with
a broken neck. The last time I went back
to my old home town I bumped into him

at the pedestrian crossing where he once fell.
Having got back on his wheels the local paper
front-paged him and the mayor, head bowed at the kerbside,
honouring his sacrifice of a broken hip.

Among what passes for a crowd on a country
kiwi shopping street, he smiled with pride
on his legacy of smooth asphalt and cement.
Boasting his age, turned seventy and looking well,

he was buying clothes at the sales. The bloke
with no legs, never without a lit cigarette,
had got all he needed three decades before,
finally succeeding, kippered to death.

As from Trees in Autumn

Consanguinity

My dad, with no intended irony,
repeats, At least I haven't lost my mind.
Though well into his eighties, his body
frail and failing, memory all but mined
out, the veil sometimes thins. He startles me,
exclaiming how I look like his father.
My hair back, in the glass, I too have seen
the image of the worthy George Arthur,
short-back-and-sided chartered accountant.
Though long extinct, the old man still before
me in this face. One nose and jaw extant
in three transients: brilliantined Great War
survivor, chook farmer and long-haired me,
partaking of one shared heredity.

House of Confinement

My father it seems strode out scot-free
where others were held confined,
escaping first his mother's house
of sober provident stone and slate
to knock about with mates that she
would never on earth
    as it is in heaven see.

School commandeered, through
back-to-backs he flew free. Knew
well his friend's housecoated mother,
innocent, though, of the need in which
she lay and sat each day with another
fee-paying 'uncle' taking tea.

Taught Sunday school as a teen,
but thought so little of The Book –
of biblical proscription – that, when
one day caught short, wiped a clean
goodbye to scriptural stricture, and –
father's clout staving off conscription –
followed his heathen heart to the land.

Through the sixties, camp commandant,
he strode the stacked hells, cages crammed
with the damned, his bird charges,
inured to watery sentiment, tarred,
debeaked, culled and slaughtered –
no thought of Nuremberg.

Overseas to New Zealand where porter
he walked a new freedom through wards.
barefaced he fled to another's bed,
debased wedded life, leaving his wife
to bleed and burn in resentment,
in time, to return, unrepentant.

Now from a home, from an aged flock
of white-haired chooks, he slips away,
roams free range, sometimes trips
and falls, knocked out and grazed,
earns a hospital stay, but, evading
the dementia cage,

    lives to leave another day.

Unique Voice

I seek to pass unseen, fugitive son
returned as tourist, certain place names
circled on unscaled maps.   After a life away,

I thought to bring no other offering
than these ashes, a daughter returned.
She who one brief span ago brought her son

home to raise on that same good loam
whose savour, in bone, blood and marrow,
she bore and I share.   Neither Wath

Cottages, nor slate and stone well, nor the house
where Mum dwelled as a lass, nor All Saints,
beneath whose weathercock uncles, suited,

to confettied aunts wed, nor stones
that mark them dead, speak as does the beck
in spate, spill-full of English rain.   Car window

down, exploring.   A rush of falling water.
North Country cataract from a pond hidden
beyond hedge and chain link fence transports

me back. Smooth fluid syllables of spillage,
surging down a concrete sluice,
usher me into infancy's skin, summoning

a black and white, box Brownie image
more vivid than memory of less-than-
one-year-old me enthroned on Prestige pram,

with hand-knit Tam o'Shanter perched atop
an infant's bonnie blank face, purging six
decades' wilful denial of my village.

A Visit with My Father

I was with my father again last night,
roommates in a rest home or Buddhist retreat –
unthinkable though either of those might
be. I open my eyes to find him seated

on the bed opposite, a shaver
in his hand, more surprised at myself sleeping
late. No hug. He's not been away for
long. We say our good mornings and I keep

thinking, how weird is this? me dreaming,
but knowing I am. 'I'm already shaved
and dressed,' he says, the encounter seeming
convincing, every bit as vivid

as waking life. Wearing a sports jacket,
collar and tie, he looks great. No longer
wasted, younger by thirty years, back in
good shape. His shoulders are broad and strong, the

former healthy glow and fullness restored
to his face – he got so cadaverous
towards the end. During the last four
months, I have often spoken of

his death using soft words, non-distressing
phrases, like 'passed away' or 'deceased'.
Given it is Dad I am addressing
I am blunt. It seems the right way to speak.

'You're dead,' I say. He doesn't seem shocked or
surprised, just tolerant, as in life,
when proselytised by the obnoxious
husband of Mum's close Christian friend (the wife

we all thought a saint.) Though disbelieving,
Dad lets me talk, the same as he does folk
who try to sell him God. Without seeming
down on Buddhism I know he hopes

one day I'll grow up and get over it.
When I withdrew from the long retreats,
those were the words he used, 'got over it'.
He was glad for me, as if I'd finally beaten

some chronic illness, wishing me the best,
as I did him, each from his own particular
point of view. Religion for eccentrics,
cuckoo, if not psychiatrically

ill. He had no truck with dreams either, said
they were mind 'freewheeling', and wouldn't like
this one. Though, with the window by his head,
he has only to turn to see the light.

Impermanence

Astronomical distances, the age
of rock, that the continents are drifting,
hard to compass – which soul wants the ground they
judged eternally beneath them shifting? –

such facts demand too much. That nothing stays
the same undoes us. Witness the fury
evolution sparks in its foes, their rage
it dare oppose an old Jewish story.

Impermanence seemed an obvious truth
when first I heard it taught, though yet to lose
a close one or love, barely out of youth,
death still distant. Since then I've known friends choose

to end their lives and others die of drink,
a stillbirth, a divorce, my mother take
a grand mal seizure, slip my grip and sink
beyond sight into a deep, dark and wake-

less ocean and my father by degrees
shed so much bodily and mental heft
that, as from trees in autumn withered leaves
take flight, one morning grown so slight he left

like breath on the breeze.
Nothing stays the same.

One Grain of Sunblood

Prospecting

The boy, heedless of the cold,
roams the north-western shore's wet sand,
sea-tumbled glass and shell treasures held
pressed to his chest in wind-numbed hands.

Grown older, I, withdrawn from the ocean,
inland, am still drawn to button, coin or bead,
found flotsam among grass, to silt my pocket,
but favour now a more notional quest.

Waking and wading from sleep to desk,
my morning unmuddied by need,
to pore over word-gravelled pages,
seeking a trace of placer gold.

Days spent and gained
extracting from coarse sand
a mustard seed's measure, one grain,
of sunblood to rest in my hand.

Blackbird, Stunned

Slam! right next to my head, a bird, full-stopped
by a window, drops stunned onto the deck,
tries to stand but, failing, falls back limp, propped
on fanned feathers, legless and listing. Neck

not fractured I guess.   Palms together in
reflex sotto voce recitation,
I witness the life in his eyes fading.
The brute persistence of respiration

transporting me back to a fatal head
injury in Emergency Room One.
Though accorded respect proper for one dead,
his lungs' lust for labour not yet quite gone.

He had jumped. The illusion of free flight
crushingly curtailed.   On the bird I seek
signs of bleeding. Though there are none, the light
behind his eyes falters and dims. His beak

shuts and breathing seems to cease. How long must
I hold my hands folded like this? Winded
in sympathy, tasting blood from a blow
to the face, praying in earnest for I don't

know what, surcease of pain or passage to
a better place? Some minutes pass. Life hangs
uncertain, the ability to stand
suddenly regained, then another Bang!

This time a lesser clumsy bump on glass.
recoiling from a magpie alighting,
quardle-ardling its mates not to pass
up on victuals unequal to fighting

back. I leap to redress the odds, deny
vicious opportunists their delight in
easy meat, gesticulating at the 'pie
with clods in my fisted hands to see the

butcher off. The would-be victim stops
one minute before, with doubtless ringing ears,
bruised brain and memory loss, he nonetheless
hops nimbly to the edge, flies off and disappears.

Grand Final

Walking the dog
during the second of that year's
two grand finals.
Floodplain parkland,
footy field and road through
unnaturally quiet,
but for the encircling roars,
rage and delight escaping half
a hundred ridge-top lounge room doors.

I remember nothing of the score
or who won the cup,
but as the horn blew
a cool change came up.
I saw the first gust,
witnessing a thing not seen before –
pine trees touched and doubled.
Departing pollen spores,
just for that moment,
ghost forms afloat
in red-tinged dust.

Seven Balloons

I raise the blind to a hot-air balloon
ascending on a gentle northerly.
Six more float to the same great height, a bloom
of airy medusas in mimicry
of the Big Dipper, sevenfold Ursa's
distant suns painted a faint monochrome
by light from the eastern sky.   I nurse a
fondness for flight, the sight of globe and glow,
silent, high and slow above the suburbs'
hurtle, or so low the full-throated roar
of their propane inferno may be heard
blazing overhead, calling me outdoors
to gaze at red giants grazing tree and
roof, coelenterates collapsing on land.

Shade Tree

The young elm resembling a child's drawing,
Green ball on a brown trunk – foliage spring
Crayoned unsprung on a lollipop stick –
Stands in the park at the end of the street,

This neither the land nor now the era
For trees from temperate 'Home', even here,
The rubicund continent's greenest rim,
The sun as soon as it first touches stings.

Increasingly ravaged by years of heat,
Seared limbs wither and fall, stripped, barked and bleached,
To lie like bones. The newest growth clings weak
Below, springing faint in a close green wreath.

Sporting, as a quarter century's growth,
Two contrasting spheres, drawn as hungry ghosts,
One brittle and dry, the other – despite
Years of crisped grass, baked dust and fire – not quite.

The drier stands broad and tall, like bleached hands
Caught cupped in a supplicatory cage.
Sprung below, the lesser globe, enfeebled
By thirst, does not thrive, but nonetheless grows.

Two interwoven shades, sharing one post.
The survivor, for all it's lost, pours all
It has been into being what it is,
Untroubled by the shadow of its past.

Smith Street

Thursday 8 January 2015

Lorne. After lunch. Everyone naps but me,
left to appreciate the eastward view
alone. Along the coast the sky, the sea
and distant promontory pale, seen through

a veil of fine drizzle. Two birds alight.
The male's crest a raffish scarlet. Their calls
a song of pulled corks. In Pizzey and Knight
the date, handwritten in pencil, records

Gang-gang cockatoos observed long prior
to this visit. Wool-gathering I lay
the guidebook by, look idly at the sky
above the farther side of Louttit Bay,

mountainous with fleece. Eucalyptus trees
frame the vista. Gum leaves hang listless, furled
for sleep. Droplets, unstirred by any breeze,
drift unhurried down on a drowsing world.

An hour takes its time elapsing. Cars pass,
but at a crawl and are few. Cloud banks low
over Aireys Inlet roll out to Bass
Strait, their procession glacially slow.

The details I gaze through slip clean away –
door, deck, trees and vegetation. At rest,
lost in contemplation of silver-grey
distance, life at its postprandial best.

Sounds of Silence

Four-thirty a.m. The world well asleep.
Not even the breathing of overnight freight
seeps in to breach my solitude. Unfolded screen
and the votive glow of lamps illuminates a field
of mute golden gazes. In writerly need
I supplicate the swan-enthroned lutanist Muse.
Through the hush between my dronings
the hard drive thrumming my desk's acoustic shell
misperceived as the night machine's rush,
sweeping through nearby streets. Wicks seethe
and spit as if possessed. The seeming
distant screaming of a grounded jumbo jet
merely an inward manic Renfield –
spider-eating thrall of the undead –
raving in my ear's padded cell.

Text Message

Beneath – a thousand morning voices –
    car, van, truck, bike, bus and ute.
Above…speech suspended,
    spaced across a pale blue page,
a lit, aloof ellipsis:
    balloon – balloon – balloon.

The Castle on the Hill

Worlds from the Très Riches Heures'
    Limewashed citadels,
The hospital – a siren's blare away –
    Stands, inglorious,
        Sans battlements or banners,
Yet claiming the heights
    And herself heir to sov'reign powers.

For all her healing virtue,
    Plain as tile behind her mask and gown
        Of grown suburban green,
Roof penuriously penned
    With figures of mast,
        Dish antenna, vent and flue,
Unfriendly bean counter's line for a view,
The scene, at least, richly cast
    Against that same vast cerulean,
        Duc de Berry blue.

The Order of Birds

Lorikeets, swift past my window, piping
shrill distraction. Drawn from dawn devotions,
my attention shifts to birds alighting
on an ornamental imitation

hill, an oriental arborvitae,
its domed topiary cupola lush
as a well-tended orchard. Parrot cries
quieted by felled constellations, hush

on stellate cones descended numberless
as nighttime stars. Plumage thrown into high
relief by light ascendant, luminous
against the backcloth of a bruise-blue sky.

No tropical bloom may vie with such quills.
Yellow, flaming orange-red, cobalt blue
and feasting beak to beak they take their fill,
devouring the exotic plenitude

of a suburban backyard. Returning
to myself and to this bird in hand, my
votive practice, imagery burning
potent still. Not surprised so much by

Leo's garden seasonally raided,
as that a moment's sight so modifies
perception: parrot head and belly reds
and blues become the hues I visualise.

Title

Two doors down drivers take a hard
Right and leave our street behind,
Speeding away, skirting and blind to
The adjacent, suburban, Scots pine-
Needle-carpeted, dog-promenade.

Parkland, ridge reached across by roots,
Rearing up exposed as long ribs,
Knots and knuckles, pterodactyl wing-
And finger-bones. Roots burred flat
By tractor mowers, rings on show,
No longer growing, smooth, weathered,
Silver-white patens, inlaid in turf.

The track's dirt terraced and criss-crossed
By sculpted wood, reminiscent
Of Daibutsu temple steps, carpet railed
By roots, as if artfully laid out.
Path beaten by a steady stream
Of feet. Earth worn bare.
Muddy when wet. In forty-degree heat,
Turned flour fine. The pines exotic, and,
Since the last drought, in decline.

This shoulder among river flats,
Before the carving of the cartographic knife,
Long tracked in song, inscribed on
And cherished by a lineage of minds as map;
Land, song and inhabitants one.

Striding the ground, well-shod and inured
To modern-day noise; outsider, knowledge
Flawed and unentitled. Even so, I wonder,
If attentive, might I wake to that lost line of song,
Take to other, and more lasting joys
And ways of wandering
Than in thrall to a plastic card.

Two Balloons

Behind the pine-treed horizon
two balloons,
like baubles, hang, barely moving,
unaccustomed oven-mitt silver
reflecting fistsful of sun.

Their light lost to layers of cloud,
the two grow menacing,
Hadean crows
glowering,
black, over houses of healing.

The iron image burns red hot,
in need of form,
in need of blows,
fingers on a forge of keys,
hammering.

A Bowl of Betrayal

Vineyard War Graves

Walking a woodland track with friends and dogs
rounding a bend, we crest a rise and see
land come into view, recently fenced off,
on the far flank of a sheltered valley.

Under raw winter light, row upon row
of posts in precise geometric lines,
ranks, files and diagonals fanned out in
support of a host of vulnerable vines.

That devotees of Bacchus and brother
god Ares should pour libations of wine
and shed blood, so unalike each other,
odd, while aligning alike grave and vine.

The same ordered tranquillity, the same
close attention to layout accorded
pine uprights and viniferous crop as
tens or hundreds of thousands of war dead.

In the Belly of a Giant Whale

The snap of banners. Brides deprived of more
than bridal gowns, married to the desert.
War victims piled in the ribbed belly of
Leviathan. The sky a pyre-burnt brown.

A congregation, their features taut, skin
drawn back in a pharaoh's leathern grin. Bones
and teeth unearthed beneath an ancient church.
A chalice, Invictus, its precious stones

forever bound in bonds of hand-wrought gold.
Union for a time wholly transcending
all embodiment. Sheaves turned to ash in
stooks of flame, restored as loaves, upending

cause and effect. All that is consumes or
is consumed, from silk to Himalayan
summits. The compass of miraculous
wounds traded for a bowl of betrayal.

Kelipotic puppets contrived of what
might have been menschen, hollowed out, vitals
vanished, neither swallowed by a Thiepval
trench of doubt nor blighted by survival.

By the Numbers

After sappers, tunnelling two years,
have finally placed, 'A million pounds',
the website reads, 'of ammonite',
and two weeks' pounding by shell,
at zero three hundred hours and ten,
June seventh, nineteen seventeen,
nineteen mines, in sequence,
ignite, 'with complete success'.

    Nothing left of the German first line at Messines.
The first and largest mine,
ninety-one thousand pounds,
eighty-eight feet beneath Lone Tree Hill,
erupts fifteen seconds late.

    The Ulstermen so killed memorialised
    by a two-hundred-and-fifty-foot crater,
    later filled to a depth of forty feet:
    the 'Pool of Peace'.
None of which concerns the ammonite,
a shelled mollusc, long extinct,
lost, with seventy-five per cent of species,
to a six-mile-wide bolide that fell
on Chicxulub Day, sixty-six MYA.
Messines, in comparison, less than a fraction
of a speck of a scintilla,
though heard, it is said, by Lloyd George
in Downing Street, and as far away
as Dublin,
the largest explosion made by Man
until Manhattan,
till Japan, the greatest killer.

Ten thousand sons, dead.
The unchecked spell-checked spelling
of Ammonal as fossil shell, not to mar telling
of 'one of the most gallant actions of the war'.

Prothesis in the Park

The once-heroic figure moulders where
he fell, ensepulchred in air beneath
tar-black pines, professional mourners, their
limbs bent in Attic attitudes of grief
over the deceased. Disarmed, bark shield shed,
innards crumbling, though bulking greater dead
than any yet standing. Unknown numbers
burrow in the slow-burning rot – their home
a moist hulk of lichen-spotted lumber,
laid out and softly returning to loam.

Renegade

I see a space and reverse my agèd Civic
to find myself pre-empted by a Renegade.
Setting my jaw, I guide my rear towards its grille.
The driver's window opens, he leans out and shouts,
'Do yer want me to go yer, 'cause I will?'

Like his vehicle he looks to be on steroids.
Reading the signs, I quickly select 'the better
part of valour', and, feeling like a mouse, drive on.
The memory of that brief encounter floods me still
with the will to spill his blood. Though six years have gone

by, I would love to shove my car door in his face,
get out and take a steering wheel lock to the lights
of his Jeep, find his house, shoot out its front windows.
I want the shit to cringe, whimpering for mercy.
This is war, between the halves of a far from whole-

hearted me, one part avoiding danger, too mild
to be caught going berko on CCTV.
He might have learnt my name, started a vendetta,
a tit-for-tat of slashed tyres, house fires, convictions
and public disgrace. If I were not a better

man I might have thrown health and sanity away,
sacrificed this ordinary life to a sick
obsession. Best I let go of, 'He stole my
parking space', but oh for the psychopathic
single-mindedness of a Keyser Söze.

Valorous

the Scots pine stands minus a limb, resin-rimed
scar three times a man's height from the ground,
on a parkland ridge one day's march behind
the lines, the planned advance to our new home. The air around

the absence abundant with bees. A black
and white bird swoops down, expertly seizing
an insect in its beak, to lift back up, settle
on a branch and set about feeding, eluding a sting.

Unfamiliar, kookaburra-like in build
and beak, time and again the bird returns to where
it saw the rift and first lined up a kill.
Repeatedly launching at blurred arrow speed, streaking
    through the air

to snatch a meaty morsel in mid-flight.
I daresay I have sighted a grey butcherbird,
direct course taken and watchfulness right.
My first impression was a pied, though of bees preferred

as prey there is no word in the guide.
My eye aligned I stare precisely placed to see
the chainsawed slice edge on. Weaving,
bees alight, silhouettes against the sky, or leave released at speed

into shimmering air heated by the lungs
of a honey-glutted beast, digesting
the nectar feast of myriad tongues.
Comrades cypress, larch and cedar fallen in the fight contesting

heat and drought, of their defeat no sign
save raw and bleached wood. If this tree could see
it would stare a thousand yards. Wounds aside
the veteran, verdant and vital yet, abides
>   far above the transient housed and hived,
>   fleeting birds and me.

Lunar Sea of Rhyme

Water of Life

Verse – when it comes out right – all the fine-grained
    cognitions garnered from time's threshing floor
unbagged, fermentation vat vaster than

any one bright sparking skull-bound sponge may
    comprehend, life, from most gross to subtlest,
distilled, the ignition of pure spirit.

On the Beach

Insanity, surely, to wake at four,
the moon's last quarter in the east, rising
to pore over refinement of line, choice
of word, while night conducts its vacant trudge.

The distant roar beyond the blind,
a voice barely heard, ignored amidst
the hiss of inner surf. No man at his desk,
intent on writing verse, dare ask more than this.

Resentful and averse to diurnal employment,
yearning for some share of time – instead
of blighted, tasked with earning – immersed
in enjoyment of a lunar sea of rhyme.

Chrome-plating the Tail Fins

Two ways the wings supporting every art
in flight, be it arrow, verse or spirit:
wild intuition inspiring the heart

and domesticated reason; target
bullseyed by feel or with recurve carbon
fibre bow and sight; the snowbound hermit's

votive song or scriptorial jargon.
Most labour like mules; few are those who play
extempore. Wretched hand be pardoned

for not taking down a poem on its way
barrelling across the land. Amazed
by Mrs Woolf, able to sense 'this wave

in the mind'. Obliged to peel each phrase
I make apart, receptive though I am
to pattern, nonetheless required to raise

such craftsmanlike refinement as I can,
till each line reflects my aim like sunlight
on the fletching of a sixties sedan.

Semi-retired

Lined and used-up, the woman
    my colleague has become.
Golden brown complexion,
    now crumpled brown paper,
        her stature shorter,
    body once-gracile
        now bird-boned.

Eighteen years since necessity
    placed us in the same arena.
Single-handedly she wrestled
    her mortgage, fought it off.
Mettle now tarnished, like a mirror;
    like me, declined to fewer shifts
        a week. I wonder at the cost.

Work on poetry, Pound advised,
    as on anything else –
    though, thank God, it's not,
    how to comply?
Land some tremendous fish,
    fill a little boat with victory,
        punch-packed, petal-soft?

How to hook a haul like that?
    Walking, vitality spent,
        with dog and notebook?
Or well-rested
    under a street-lit, big-city sky,
        blackbird trilling up
    a day of uninterrupted solitude?

Too much time alone,
    a long way still from trance-
        scribing the Muse.
My shrinking horizon
    engenders only obsession,
        attempts to keep house,
    papers and laundry
organised,
        shoes and words
        in line.

Sacred Text

Rereading again Heaney's thirty-four
    poems in his Death of a Naturalist
        I am overcome. About to touch the
Faber and Faber volume to my fore-
    head, I catch myself and stop in mid lift,
        curtail the inappropriate gesture.
Despite my ardent admiration for
    his work, and though well worthy of respect,
        this is not a Mahāyāna Sūtra.

Englamoured

Parent Birds

Two patient parent birds stand,
Building their nest, so impossibly slow
That they seem not to move.
Cranes, in attentive attitudes,
Taking such pains, lifting each strand,

Adding bit by bit to the structure,
That in a long afternoon five or six
Lengths of stick, no more, are lifted
Into place. Months taking shape.
The pieces, hoisted, hang on lines

Drawn so fine that at the distance
Of a thousand paces, against
An increasingly portentous sky,
They are hard to detect.
By the time the workday is done

The construction – a dense, woven
Cube, a mesh of rigid lines,
Everything straight lines – is filled
With illuminated hyphens.
Only now, in the premature gloom,

Does their constant fluoro glow
Show, bars of yellow light,
And the infestation of orange
Fleas ease off and disperse.
The birds are still, silhouettes fading

Against advancing storm and dark,
Seeming unperturbed by the growing
Threat of lightning strike and another night
Spent stiffly waiting, unwarmed
By their nest's interior light.

Sylvan Vision

A mountain ash stands amidst hills blackened
by its dark green kin, beside a bridle path
on Mount St Leonard. This one among many
revealing to a moment of enhanced

imagination the mystery within
its skirted trunk: light as liquid honey coursing
through eucalyptus leaves and branches
to a tankful of canopy-dappled sap.

Inside a figure hangs, suspended
as in amber, face upturned, expression rapt,
limbs flung out, sunk deep in sweet, abandoned
cessation of the need to breathe or think.

Such an idyll, but a dryad in rural
Australia? Feeble mimesis of Greek myth.
As for Saint Leonard, pious mediaeval
fiction acclaimed for freeing from their varied bonds

captives, women in labour and plague-smitten
cattle. Why this denial of traditional story
and station, an inappropriate top-hatting
by white men? This presiding mountain rightly

headman, warrior or grandfather deity.
Character best demonstrated by long-standing
choice in raiment, wind-driven hail and burning
bush, my own faerie fancies notwithstanding.

Vajrayogini

Circling the sun, cameras capture
the fleeting image of a tornado,
a miniscule twist of solar flame
sufficiently great, were she close,
to incinerate Earth, not merely blister
her surface, burn trees and grass,
but blast rock back to plasma – the state
before the planet fell together –

all life in an instant, extinct.
Incandescent vision of heavy weather,
swift-rotating blender-blades from hell,
demonesque dance of heliospheric fire.
One ravening cell on the sun's facial skin.
Conflagration safe to admire
as one might depictions
of the dakini,
similarly fulminant,
energetic, spinning red
at the distance of oriental art.

Third-eyed, fanged protector,
she who, barefoot and naked, hair flying wild,
skirted and festooned in swirling ropes of bone,
highland flings, skullcup held high,
brimful of bliss-bestowing nectar,
flaying knife poised to confer loss
of ego, that which never was.
Sol's same raw radiance taken
to another plane. Her nature and offer divine,
her krater a crucible in which to dare
to lay and wake as free of self
as sunlight is of dross.

Four Balloons

On the cushion at Mattins
courting illumination
on inward beams of shining
white, red and blue,
distraction arises.

The naked light bulb burning
erotic bedroom red,
a fatuus in glass
or the branch beyond
blossoming?

A second globe, following
a season of none, brightened
by a lance of half-risen sun,
translucent against
a groundlessness of mist.

Glazed cliff face mirroring
the first and last gold shafts,
four will-o'-the-wisps,
slow above it, hearse-black
in returning dark.

Englamoured by this
procession of snares
for the unwary,
neck craned at the cortège
of concentration passed.

Banshee

Agitated and restless, the night
    sets wind chimes ringing.
A man, visited by dreams of collapse,
    of chest caved in
by falling timber, cries out,
    waking his wife.
Shaking, barely able to aim her
    finger, she taps the screen
to summon an ambulance
    shrieking to the attack,
an ululating hag
    straddling the air,
a banshee keen to save –
    or is it claim – a life.

The Consequence of Line

Chops

My first chop – name in seal characters – came
from a street vendor in Tibet, the stamp
a functional, red rubber knob, its face
just less than one inch square. The maker sold

his work from a board laid across the seat
and handlebars of a sit-up-and-beg
parked standing in a Lhasa marketplace.
No language in common, he asks me what

characters I would like incised. I speak
my two names, twice. He asks, 'Again?' With eyes
closed and forehead creased in concentration,
he cocks his head and listens. I pronounce

the words taking care to articulate
each syllable clearly, while watching him
struggle to transcribe the outlandish sounds
I make as a workable inscription.

Turned now in my fingers the artefact,
utilitarian if not ugly,
offers its hand-carved base as evidence
of patience and skill. Logograms sculpted

sharp and proud amidst a field of lines, fine
furrows expertly ploughed with a scalpel
blade. Though he caught my name askew, his hand
nonetheless true to what he heard through

the filter of dialect. A friend fluent
in Chinese reads 'Lai cha Lai ga lai' and
laughs. Twenty years pass. I find Mr Lee
online before our trip to Singapore,

show him characters I wanted inscribed
on soapstone I had had for almost that long.
Having made some changes to my design
he says, 'Come back tomorrow,' and, donning

protective gear, sets to work, engraving
in an hour by machine what once took days
of painstaking labour to fashion by
hand. Unlike my mother-in-law and wife

Mr Lee does not pose questions. I could
not have answered them any more than why
I bought the stamp, over-priced in the first
place, from a hotel gift shop in Xining:

an iconic male guardian lion,
ball beneath forepaw, muscular, curly-
maned and snarling, its weighty translucence
pleasing to both palm and eye. Since bringing

the souvenir home I've barely used it.
To set such a seal on even the best
of verse feels pretentious, calling to mind
the fury of art teacher Mrs Last

at my defacement of a promising
pencil sketch, adding the stylised A.D.
of Albrecht Dürer. Some moment had passed.
Whatever talent she had glimpsed in me

would long lie dormant till I came to share
her view, that of all past masters of fine
art, or seal cutters, their opinion, their
creed, confirming the consequence of line.

Fondue

The ocean of molten cheese you've prepared
is news to me, and the retro forks and pot
in flame enamel. Bought from where? I stare,

but not for long. We share a baguette, not
cut too thin. I expect, on dipping in,
to raise bread laden and dripping with hot

clumps of Gruyère, but am surprised by thin,
Kirschwasser-watered, alcoholic soup.
My slice sopping. Luxuriating in

the taste, we moan as we eat as we scoop.
Bread all but flying from our plates, we find
the French loaf fast running out, are reduced

to digging with five-day-old crusts for rind.
The best coming last. Great glutinous globs
of Camembert mould, bringing to mind

an anti-smoking ad: reliable gloved
hands against a medical man's white coat,
squeezing ripe atherosclerotic sludge

from the congealed plumbing of a smoker.
Concealing my thoughts, I enjoy, to the last
heart-stopping clot, a dish I hope not to die for.

Show Business

The boulevarded bank of the summer Seine,
Rive Gauche sights, Plane tree shade.
By the chest-high, ashlar wall,
inches from my shoe, I spot a shine.
Before I can stake my claim a woman swoops,
figure from postcard-view ground,
puncturing my personal space.
Scooping up the thing she game show hosts
a ring in my face, fortune-telling
my mother tongue, effervescing
'Your lucky day!'
and pressing on me winnings.
My arm lifts.
I look askance at the buttery, baby-doll charm
placed to pose on my palm,
let it sit. Take stock of face,
hair and good enough dress.
Dissimulation, close up,
not disguising eyes, first-night wide,
nor her marginal look.
Having done her professional Ariel best
to raise a minor tempest of covetousness
she takes one beat's rest.
I frown at the stagy feel of this supernormal
annulus, too wide around,
bold as brass cuckoo egg.
Isn't there some scam?
Furtive burnishing, street thaumaturgy
invoking Avarice to make her own gold mine
and herself, transmuted, richer.

Keeping mute, disowning distance
I place the ring on stone.
Moments ago gushing my fortune
found, she turns the faucet off, falls
silent, reclaims her lure and, without rushing,
is chameleon gone.
Too slow I turn to the broad promenade, find
walkers few and all anonymous. Of the sham
alchemist no sign, her act successful in vanishing
back into the picture.

Green Grocer

Cyclochila australasiae

The passage of a leaf descending, tracked
at the edge of vision. The hard crispness
of its impact – a small papery smack –
demanding, What package is this, witnessed

falling at my feet? A cicada, laid
immobile on ungenerous gravel,
torpid with cold.   Intending aid
I tender a twig.   Able to grapple,

its hooked feet grip, take hold to hang
inverted. This fat beakful of meat
unhurt, disguised so well no magpie looks
to eat it.   Lifted to the feeble heat

of sunlight cast on a camellia bush,
camouflaged khaki evading surprise
revitalised by the caffeine rush
of solar calorification. Two eyes

café au lait, a third gold-flecked
amber. Miniature, cellophane-clad
Martian; armoured and compact. Fake-
Fabergé netsuke in olive drab.

Avant-garde Performance

Ratcheting the sun. Morning bruised
by her throttle's rasp and crake. Spurred,
yawning, into being. Abused,
I wake to the world and the wattlebird,

wishing her gone. Hackles raised
at her disdain of my right
to rest, unimpressed by displays
of aerobatic skill. Alighting

on the kylix's lip, she glances
my way, tongue out, nectar-sipping
the waters. Taking no chances,
watchful for stalkers, dipping

her keel in shallows of yellow-brown
rain. Bathing belly-deep in
dilute dirt. Darting up, then, fleetingly, down
again. Retreating

with a snap of the wing. She stays
one second, tantalising, sure
of herself as elusive – prey,
despite a lack of predator,

constantly checking. Thus engaged
she curtly rejects my displeasure
with one breve, composed by John Cage,
croaked among crab apple boughs, and leaves.

Elation Muted

On my knees in the entry, tweezing knots
of grass, their growth deemed unseemly for a
property on sale. Weed-free drive a fright,
like the sight of newly healed 'work' on an

ageing face, bringing starkly to mind the
patient I, as a nursing student, was
once called upon to view, anaesthetised,
draped in theatre green, unidentified.

Between her splayed, Sudanese thighs displayed,
a smooth obliteration.   Merciful Muse!
may I never excise from my verse
one humble, surplus-seeming syllable,

lest it likewise lose that keenest pleasure
in connection. Cant about improvement
on nature veils the numbing erasure
that is, consent aside, the knife's intent.

Sinophile

Timeless, rectilinear, frosted glass,
neither less nor more vogue, modernist or
now than in any year, future or past:
the lamps we imported from Singapore.

Things Chinese: a daybed, said to be one
hundred and thirty years old; rosewood chairs;
timber screens and panels hung in windows
and on walls; blue ceramic birds, a pair

standing erect as if to guard from turned
up roof tiles a Forbidden City street
corner; foo dogs, two on a table firm
and low enough to function as a seat;

a cabinet, china gathering dust
behind its latticework; the courtyard's tin
lanterns, above a serene stone Buddha,
their cheap perforations wishing us

double happiness; seven framed pictures
of sparrows and turtle doves perched among
blossom, painted on silk, the artist's seal
in red; a console table with horse hoof

feet; a ceramic stool in luminous
aqua; several small tables; a cupboard
held closed by an ornate brass locking pin;
a leaning stone pagoda covered in

a pleasing green patina. All in all
the setting for a full moon dream come true,
wine and brocade, calligraphy falling
from my hand in ink of dawn-gathered dew.

Schools of Style

Stratigraphy

Contemplating the way things rise and fall,
this breath, this perception, the hydraulic
hammer, every Bam! Bam! Bam! Bam! Bam!
every grain sifting down, unseen against

the grey, burying the past. Gandharan
iconographic clout gaining sway throughout
a subcontinent, mounting Himalayan
passes, carried to Tibet. Schools of style

passed through China to Japan, west to east
and back. History accumulating
on my shrine as precious scree. Formulae
and texts penned the month, the century

or millennium before last. The Raj's
vajra, chanted *bendza* in Tibet. Fibres
raised from layered Turkoman rugs settle
reddening each page of Indic script.

No end to transformation. Strata rendered
more compact with each microgram of change.
After generations thriving the Monastic
foundation in a private waiting room

mound of *Geographic*s under Afghan dust
and sand, doomed to be robbed of artefacts
and bulldozed aside. Buddhist Bactria
a Chinese copper mine, lost, Bamiyanned.

Delivery

The expression he wears, driving past, more
grim than sober. He pulls in at number
eight, my neighbour in his white van. Its rear
across the street, one half dark glass, appears

an impenetrable sheet of black ice,
cracked down the middle. He goes to his front
door with an offering of cellophane,
wrapping paper and roses, rings the bell,

stands and waits. Nothing happens. No matching
curtain moves at any window. The house,
only two years old, more than sufficient
for a couple with three or four children,

though at the moment they are planning none.
He trudges back to his driver's seat, slumps
down, gazing blankly over flowers hung
dejected from his fingers. In the house

a woman sits behind a bolted door
and obscured windows, primly titrating
the caustic taste of gall down her man's throat.
It is past eleven. He drives away

to languish, a burning in the middle
of his chest, for what remains of his day
of labour. Six hours pass. The empty van
stands in the driveway. Permitted at last

to enter, he begs her forgiveness. She
accepts the roses. They are friends again.
Nothing in this world ever goes to waste,
except perhaps for suffering and pain.

Pursuit

A predator is on safari in my room,
a small jumping spider, camouflaged and squat,
with more paired eyes than the headlights of a hunting
guide's Land Rover. I, the Serengeti sky god,

breathe sudden Sub-Saharan weather down on him
for the pleasure of seeing the arthropod spring
across my desk's printed veldt, or leave him to range
on Kilimanjaro-steep wall, window frame or

dust-bedevilled savannahs of paper and wood,
busy with my own big game, stalking among herds
of fitting words and phrases to find for my verse
an offering of living muscle, bone and blood.

At the Movies

After a climb we reach our preferred seats
in the middle of the top row. Settled
in above the hoi polloi we wait for
their noise to abate. I should know better
than to choose a Sunday afternoon to

pander to my taste in animated
movies. Cartoons are for small children. Four
people stride up the stairway towards us,
their conversation and laughter distinct,
even over a theatre full of kids.

They sit in front of us, and are as loud
as any family I've heard. Why should
I resent their obvious pleasure in
each other's company, ebullient
and friendly? Nonetheless I do. Feeling

they occupy too much space, that we are
forced to endure their presence. I suppress
my unwarranted aversion, despite
the mother's foghorned opinions, until
the son with long, lank hair, seated inches

from my left knee, sneezes. He does so, head
turned to the right, into air I might well
soon be breathing. A sneeze, wholehearted, moist
and unrestrained by tissue or linen.
His second sneeze, even more productive

than the first, is at least into his palm.
Then he confirms my already jaundiced
judgement of his level of refinement,
turning my stomach by wiping his hand
on the outside of his upholstered seat,

and the action hasn't even started.
Later, supermarket shopping, my wife
pokes me in the ribs, it's them, she whispers.
The trolley handle's feel seems suddenly
enough to lay me low with OCD.

River Red Gums

Returning before the temperature climbs
I drive ten or twelve minutes through traffic
to stare at the trunks of these river red
gums. Privileged to sit in parkland

on a rock in the cool shade of a school day
morning as mothers and children pass hand
in hand, a teen with bare arms and beanie
texts while walking to the bus stop, and the road

conveys commuters between these three-
hundred-year-old trees, eucalypts well used
to the heat about to bake this drought-prone
dirt again today. Trunks anything but

straight, limbs spastiform as if arrested
in mid-convulsion, leaves indifferent
to light, of which there is more than enough,
shy and shrinking from glare. Bark in texture,

form and colour mimetic of the land,
a scaled-down interior, river clay
in undulating lines of silver-grey
mud and eroded saffron-orange sand,

sere as sun-dried hide revealing signs of
cast off cladding as it peels, suggestive
of designs for camo under torn taupe,
or the serpentine coursing of water

over vast, flat spaces, washes of sand,
clay and gravel fanned out across a wide
desert, as if streams carved and abandoned
in a tracery of desiccation

were viewed from the sky. A range of silvers
and faded golds exposed where sinuous
strips most recently fell, the ground littered
with leather like the floor of some manic

cordwainer's cell. Free to lollygag, lost
in the texture of bark, form and colour
evoking old stone age cave-wall aurochs
and deer hand-painted in ochre and clay.

Pigment, in this unwitting work of art,
skilfully palette-knifed by that artist,
Mistress Nature. If sufficiently steeped
in this primordial aesthetic – lore

as far from easy to assimilate
as north Arnhem Land pidgin is distant
from Attic Greek – my suspicion is that
an appreciation for another,

harsher beauty might seep beneath my skin,
cockatoos as they pass shrieking overhead
already pleasing. This country's crust
scorched and fissured, its grasses seeming dead,

every mottled, particoloured flank, part-
amputated limb, each hollow and shed
branch holey with borer only augments
my admiration for the river red.

www.ingramcontent.com/pod-product-compliance
Lightning Source LLC
Chambersburg PA
CBHW070923080526
44589CB00013B/1415